After-School

Kids' Crafts

Colorful crafts are fun ways for children to make memories. With a little help from an adult, these playful projects are all quick and easy to make.

LEISURE ARTS, INC. • Maumelle, Arkansas

Butterfly Finger Puppet

Finished Size: about 5$^1/_2$" x 4"

SHOPPING LIST

***Note:** Supplies and instructions are for making 1 finger puppet.*

- ❍ craft foam in desired colors
- ❍ 4 2-hole buttons in desired color
- ❍ $^1/_2$" wide elastic
- ❍ 3" length of white cotton string
- ❍ 2 small googly eyes
- ❍ 6-strand embroidery floss in desired color
- ❍ embroidery needle
- ❍ scissors
- ❍ low-temp glue gun and glue sticks
- ❍ tracing paper

To make the Puppet

*Use needle and 6 strands of floss for all sewing. Knot 1 end of the floss. See **Tip**, to knot floss ends.*

1. Trace patterns onto tracing paper. Use the patterns to cut 1 large wings, 2 small wings, and 1 body in desired colors of craft foam.
2. Place the body in the center of the large wings. Holding the body in place, bring the needle up from the back of the large wings, through the body, and through to the back of the butterfly. Repeat to make several long stitches. Knot the floss on the back; trim the extra floss.

3. Place a button at the top of 1 small wing. Hold the button in place and carefully poke the needle through 1 of the buttonholes until it appears on the back; remove the needle. Notice a small hole on the back of the small wing. Bring the needle up from the back of the small wing through the small hole and buttonhole. Take the needle down through the second buttonhole. Stitch through the buttonholes again. Knot the floss on the back; trim the extra floss.

4. Repeat Step 3 to sew buttons to the bottom of the small wing and to the remaining small wing.

5. To attach the small wings to the large wings, place one small wing on the large wings. Attach in the same manner as Step 2. Knot the floss on the back; trim the extra floss. Sew the remaining small wing to the large wings.

6. For the antennae, glue the center of the string to the back of the body. To prevent fraying, add a small dot of glue to the ends of the string. Glue 2 googly eyes to the body.

7. Wrap a piece of elastic around your middle finger to measure your finger size; add 3/8". Cut the elastic to that length. Overlapping the ends 3/8", glue the elastic together to make a ring. Glue the ring to the back of the body.

8. To play with the butterfly, place the puppet on your middle finger. Move your pointer and ring fingers up and down underneath the butterfly to make the wings move up and down.

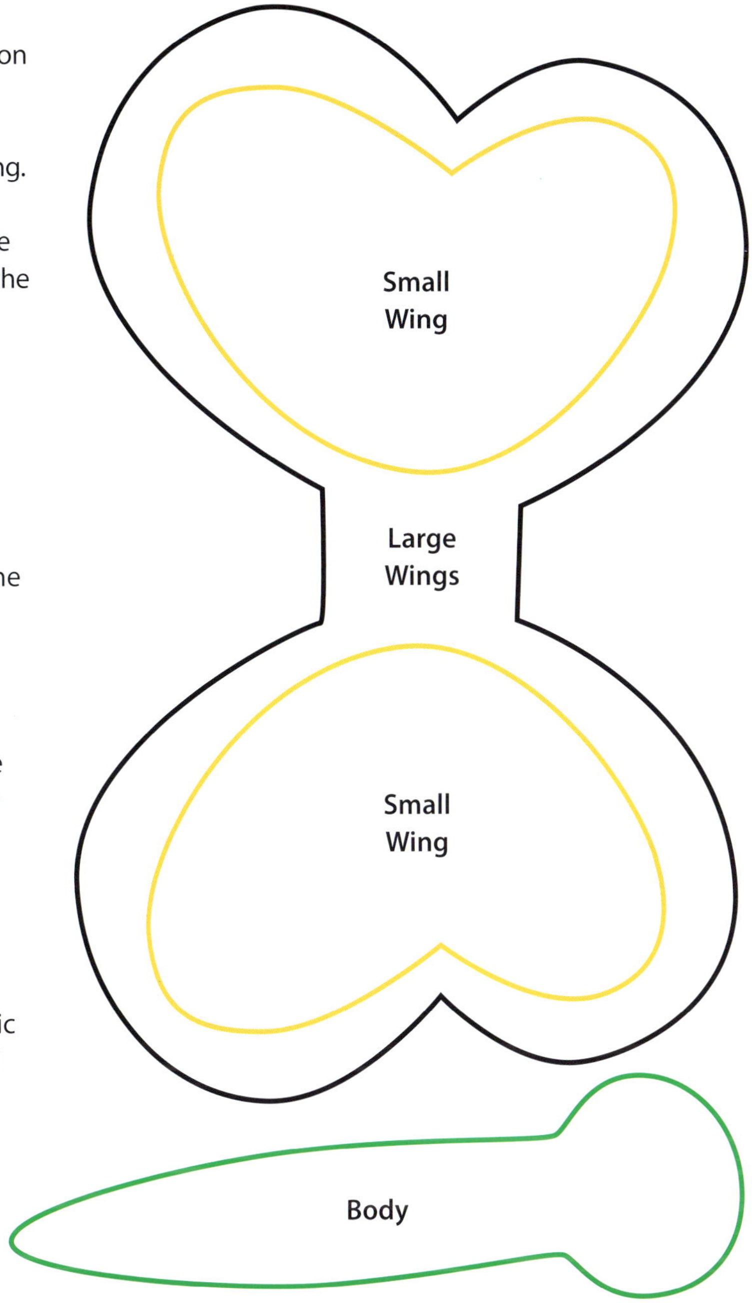

Tip:
Tying a knot at the end of the stitches:

1. Thread the needle underneath the last stitch, making a loop **(Fig. 1)**.
2. Bring the needle back through the loop **(Fig. 2)** and pull all the yarn or floss through tightly.
3. Repeat Steps 1-2 to make a knot **(Fig. 3)**. Cut off the extra yarn or floss.

Fig. 1

Fig. 2

Fig. 3

Unicorn

Finished Size: 9" diameter

SHOPPING LIST

- ❍ 9" diameter embroidery hoop
- ❍ 18" x 18" square of black cross stitch fabric
- ❍ white felt
- ❍ 6-strand cotton embroidery floss - white and black
- ❍ 6-strand rayon embroidery floss - red, pink, yellow, blue, and purple
- ❍ 6-strand gold metallic embroidery floss
- ❍ embroidery needle
- ❍ washi tape or painter's tape
- ❍ small black pony bead
- ❍ scissors
- ❍ low-temp glue gun and glue sticks
- ❍ tracing paper
- ❍ straight pins

To make the Unicorn

Use needle and 6 strands of floss for all sewing. Knot 1 end of the floss. See ***Tip****, page 3, to knot floss ends.*

1. Separate the embroidery hoop rings. Place the cross stitch fabric on top of the inside hoop and press the outside hoop over the fabric and inside hoop, pulling the fabric tight. Tighten the screw at the top of the hoop to hold the fabric in place.

2. Trace pattern onto tracing paper. Use the pattern to cut a unicorn from felt. Pin the unicorn to the fabric.

3. Starting at the bottom of the horn, use white floss and Running Stitches **(Fig. 1)** to sew around the outside edge of the unicorn. Knot the floss on the back; trim the extra floss.

4. Use gold metallic floss and Straight Stitches to sew across the horn from bottom to top. Knot the floss on the back; trim the extra floss.

5. Place a length of washi tape or painter's tape to create a line where you want to sew the mane **(Fig. 2)**.

6. For the mane, use red floss and come up from the back of the fabric at the base of the ear and sew straight stitches for about 1". Knot the floss on the back; trim the extra floss.

7. Repeat Step 6 with the pink, yellow, blue, and purple floss to complete the mane. Remove the tape.

8. Use black floss to sew the pony bead on the unicorn for an eye. Knot the floss on the back; trim the extra floss.

9. Pull the fabric tight in the hoop. Leaving about 3/4", cut off the extra fabric around the back of the hoop. Glue the fabric around the inside rim on the back of the hoop.

Fig. 1

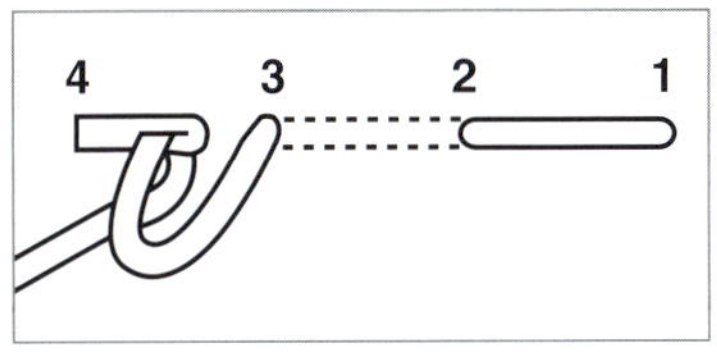

A Running Stitch consists of a series of straight stitches with the stitch length equal to the space between the stitches. Come up at 1 and go down at 2. Come up at 3 and go down at 4. Continue in this manner.

Fig. 2

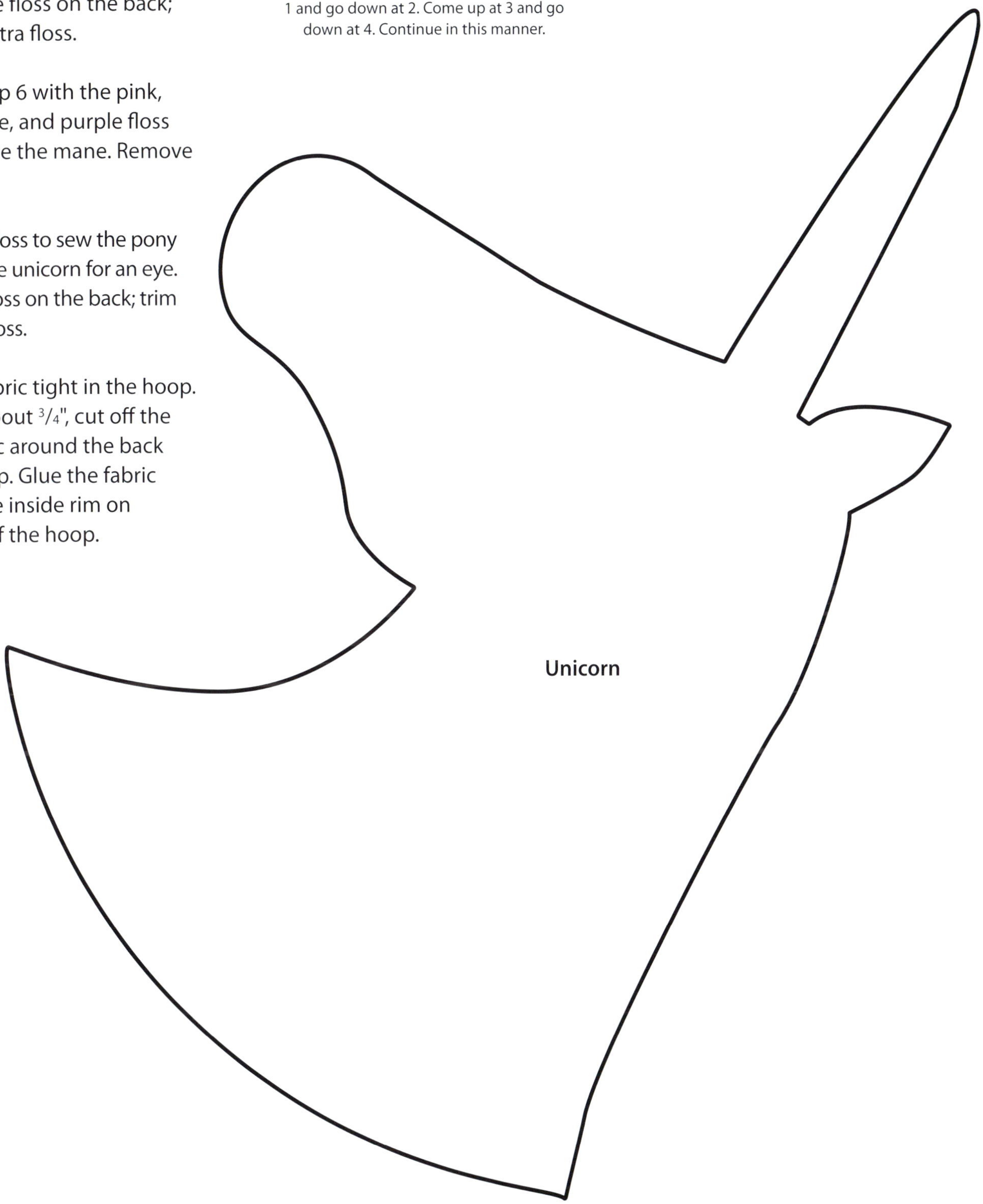

Paper Plate Mandala

Finished Size: about 10" diameter

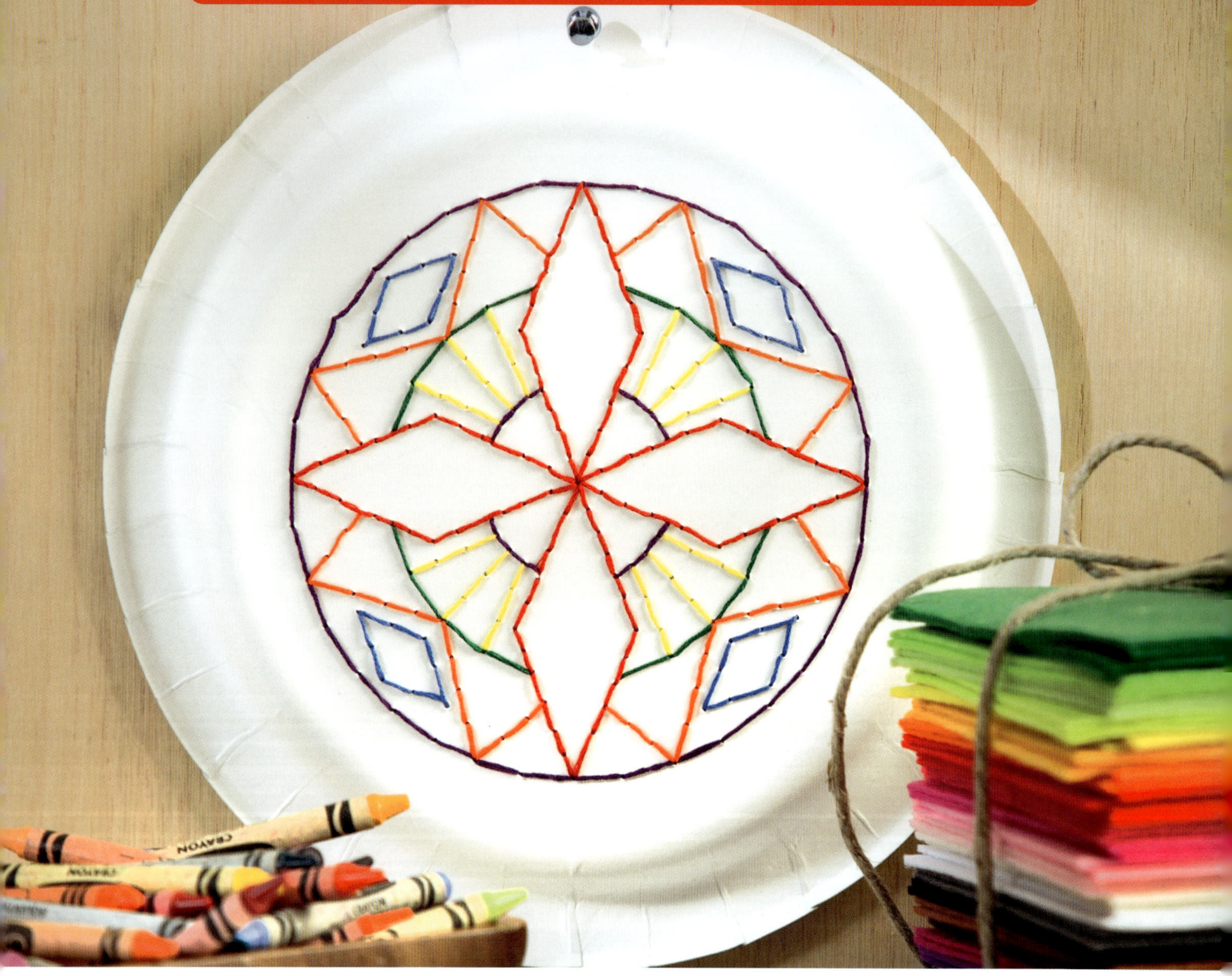

SHOPPING LIST

- ❍ heavy-duty paper plate
- ❍ glue stick
- ❍ push pin
- ❍ 6-strand embroidery floss - red, orange, yellow, green, blue, and purple
- ❍ embroidery needle
- ❍ scissors

To make the Mandala

Use needle and 6 strands of floss for all sewing. Knot 1 end of the floss. See ***Tip****, page 3, to knot floss ends.*

1. Photocopy the mandala pattern. Cut out the pattern and glue it to the front of the paper plate.
2. Use the push pin to poke holes around the pattern to mark the sewing lines. Add a hole in every corner and about 1/4" apart along each line **(Fig. 1)**. Turn the plate to the back **(Fig. 2)**.

Fig. 1

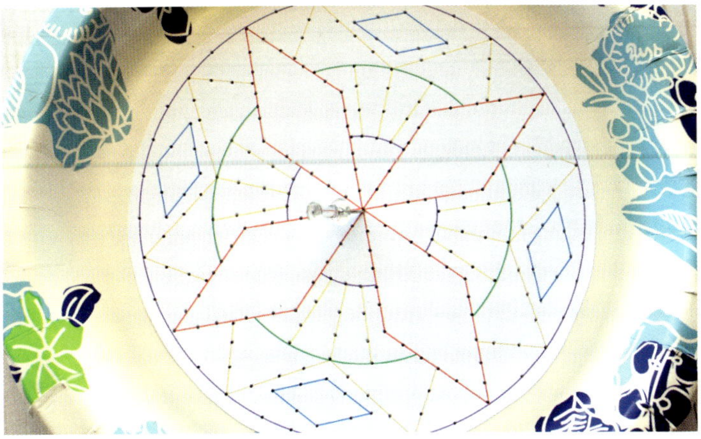

Fig. 2

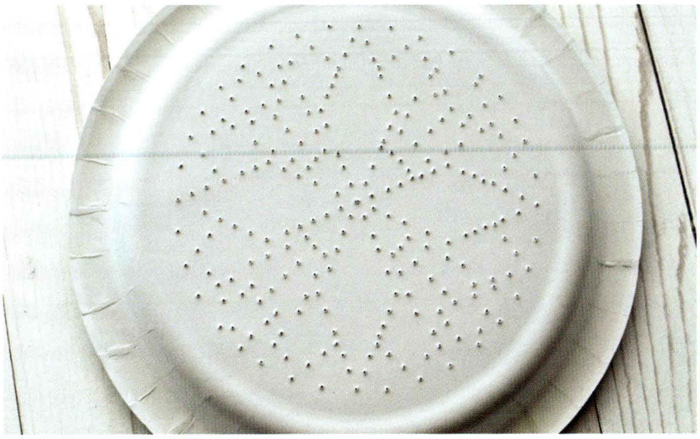

3. Using red floss, bring the needle up through one of the holes from the front of the plate along 1 red line. On the back of the plate, sew Backstitches (**Fig. 3**) along all the red lines. At the end, knot the floss on the front of the plate; trim the extra floss.

4. Continue in this manner with each color and sewing the coordinating colored shapes on the pattern with Backstitches.

Mandala

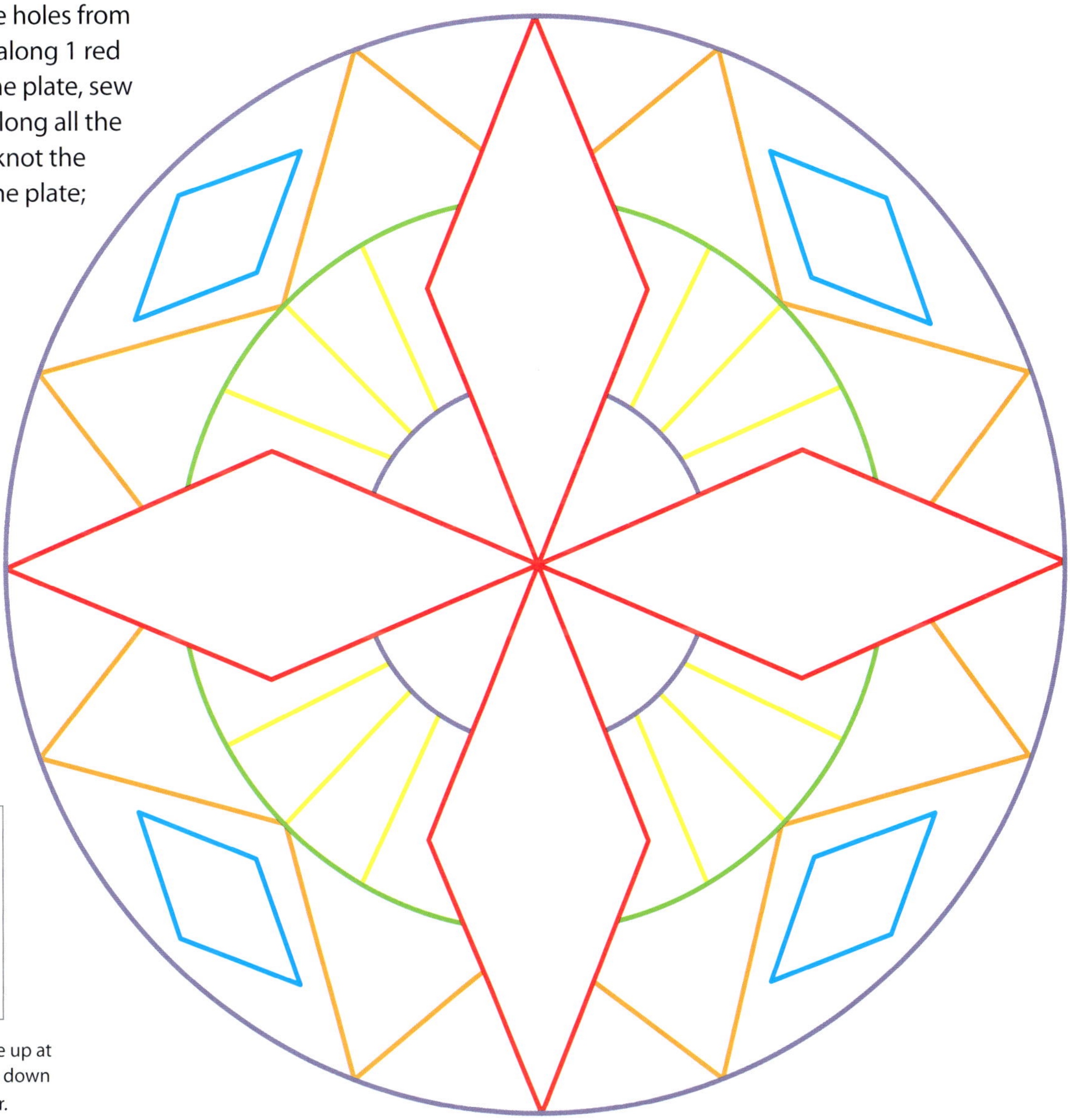

Fig. 3

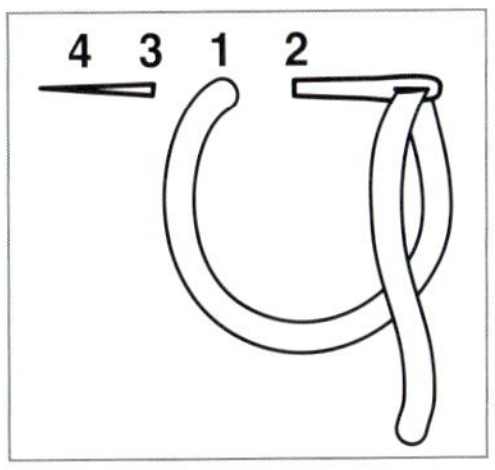

Come up at 1; go down at 2. Come up at 3; go down at 1. Come up at 4; go down at 3. Continue in this manner.

Paper Plate Flower

Finished Size: 9" x 15$^1/_2$"

SHOPPING LIST

Note: *Supplies listed are for making 1 flower.*

- ❍ 9" heavy-duty paper plate
- ❍ acrylic paints in desired colors
- ❍ paintbrush
- ❍ yellow and green yarns
- ❍ $^{3}/_{16}$" diameter wood dowel
- ❍ green felt
- ❍ blunt-pointed needle with a large eye
- ❍ push pin
- ❍ scissors
- ❍ low-temp glue gun and glue sticks
- ❍ tracing paper

To make the Flower

*See **Tip**, page 3, to knot yarn ends.*

1. Paint the outside rim of the paper plate any color you like. You can use 1 color or many colors. Be sure to let the paint dry really well.

2. Use the push pin to punch holes around the inside circle of the plate about $^{1}/_{4}$" apart (**Fig. 1**).

3. Cut about 10 feet of yellow yarn. Thread the needle; knot the other end. Bring the needle up from the back of the plate in any hole. Push the needle down through one of the holes on the front of the plate. Pull the yarn through the hole until it's kind of tight.

4. Keep sewing up and down through the holes. When you reach the end of the yarn, knot the yarn on the back of the plate; trim the extra yarn. If you run out of yarn before you have finished sewing all the holes, knot the yarn on the back and begin again with another yarn length.

5. Cut about 10 feet of green yarn. Glue one end to the yarn about 4" from one end of the dowel. Wrap the yarn around the dowel all the way to the other end. Try to keep it close together and smooth. When you get to the other end, wrap in the other direction about $^{1}/_{2}$" apart. Glue the yarn to the dowel; trim the extra yarn.

6. Trace pattern onto tracing paper. Use the pattern to cut 2 leaves from green felt. Glue the leaves to the dowel. Glue the dowel to the back of the paper plate (**Fig. 2**).

Fig. 1

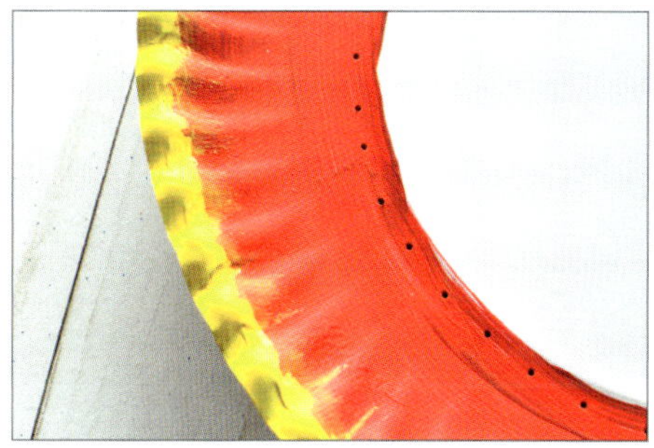

Fig. 2

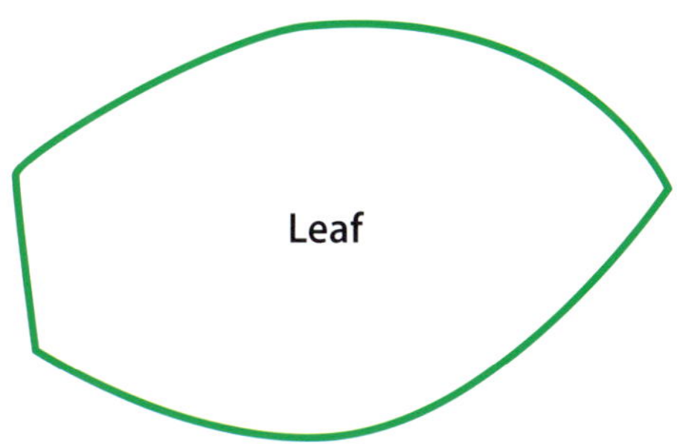

Key Chain

Finished Size: about 5 1/2" long

SHOPPING LIST

Note: *Supplies and instructions are for making 1 key chain.*

- ❍ two 1" diameter unpainted wood beads
- ❍ metallic acrylic paint - 2 colors
- ❍ paper plate
- ❍ small paper or Styrofoam™ drinking cup
- ❍ 3 paintbrushes
- ❍ 12" of leather cording
- ❍ 2 skeins of 6-strand variegated embroidery floss
- ❍ key chain ring
- ❍ scissors

To make the Key Chain

1. Use the handle of a paintbrush to poke 2 holes in the bottom of the drinking cup.

2. Pour a small amount of paint on the paper plate. Place a bead on the handle end of a paintbrush; paint the bead. Place the paintbrush in the hole in the cup; allow the bead to dry.

3. Repeat Step 2 to paint the remaining bead with the remaining paint color.

4. To make the tassel, remove the paper bands from the skeins of floss. Cut a 10" length from each skein. Lay the 2 skeins together. Tie 1 10" floss length around the center of the group **(Fig. 1)**.

5. Aligning the centers, lay the leather cording on top of the floss knot. Tie the floss tails around the leather cording **(Fig. 2)**; trim the floss ends.

6. Fold the embroidery floss group in half; bunch the floss together tightly. Wrap the remaining 10" floss length about 1" below the knot; tie a knot. Trim the floss ends **(Fig. 3)**.

7. Cut off the bottom of the floss group to the desired tassel length **(Fig. 4)**.

8. Thread the beads on the two leather cording ends; knot the cording at the top of the beads.

9. Place the ring on 1 leather cording end; tie a knot to secure. Cut off the extra cording ends.

Fig. 1

Fig. 2

Fig. 3

Fig. 4

Flower Headband

Finished Size: approximately 18" around

SHOPPING LIST

- ❍ 2" x 22" piece of green felt
- ❍ felt sheets - red, dark pink, pink, light pink, purple, and lavender
- ❍ assorted-color flower-shaped buttons
- ❍ white 6-strand embroidery floss
- ❍ embroidery needle
- ❍ 1 yard of $^3/_8$" wide white ribbon
- ❍ scissors
- ❍ measuring tape
- ❍ low-temp glue gun and glue sticks
- ❍ tracing paper

Fig. 1

Fig. 2a

Fig. 2b

Fig. 3

To make the Headband

Use needle and 6 strands of floss for all sewing. Knot 1 end of the floss.

1. Measure around your head; subtract 2". Cut a $1^1/_4$" wide green felt headband this measurement. Cut a small slit on both ends of the headband. This is where you will attach the ribbon later.

2. Trace the patterns onto tracing paper. Use the flower patterns to cut 9-12 of each flower from assorted-color felt. The number of flowers you will need will depend on the length of the headband. Use the leaf pattern to cut 25-30 leaves from green felt.

3. Place 1 upper flower on top of 1 lower flower. Add a button on top **(Fig. 1)** and place them next to the slit on 1 end of the headband; don't cover the slit. To attach the flowers and button, bring the needle through the felt and buttonhole, leaving about a 3" tail. Sew the button in place **(Fig. 2a-2b)** ending with the floss on the back of the headband. Knot the floss using the long end; trim the floss ends **(Fig. 3).**

4. Repeat Step 3 to sew all the flowers to the headband, overlapping the flowers slightly.

5. Glue the leaves around the flowers as desired.

6. Cut a piece of ribbon the length of the headband plus 18". Place the ribbon behind the headband. Place 1 ribbon end through each slit. Place the headband around your head. Tie the ribbon ends in a bow so it fits snuggly. Trim ribbon ends as desired.

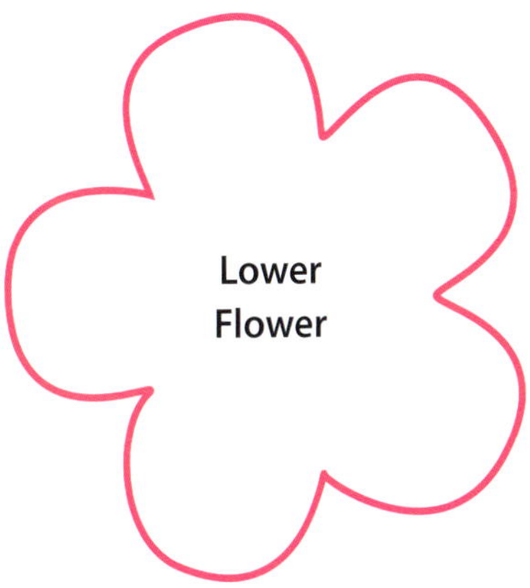

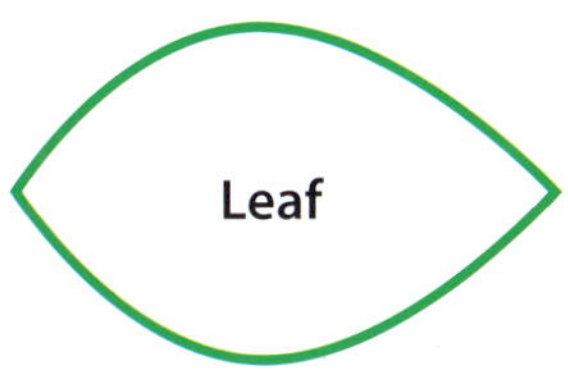

Button Tree

Finished Size: 8" diameter

SHOPPING LIST

- ❍ 8" diameter embroidery hoop
- ❍ 18" x 18" square of cream fabric
- ❍ brown felt
- ❍ assorted buttons
- ❍ white 6-strand embroidery floss
- ❍ embroidery needle
- ❍ straight pins
- ❍ scissors
- ❍ low-temp glue gun and glue sticks
- ❍ tracing paper

To make the Button Tree

*Use needle and 6 strands of floss for all sewing. Knot 1 end of the floss. See **Tip**, page 3, to knot floss ends.*

1. Separate the embroidery hoop rings. Place the fabric on top of the inside hoop and press the outside hoop over the fabric and inside hoop, pulling the fabric tight. Tighten the screw at the top of the hoop to hold the fabric in place.

2. Trace the pattern onto tracing paper. Use the pattern to cut a tree trunk from brown felt. Pin the tree trunk to the fabric.

3. To sew the tree trunk to the fabric, bring the needle up from the back of the fabric about 1/4" inside the edge of the tree trunk. Take the needle down from the front of the fabric at the edge of the tree trunk. Spacing the stitches about 1/8"-1/4" apart, repeat around the edge of the tree trunk **(Fig. 1)**. Knot the floss on the back of the fabric; trim the extra floss.

4. Sew each button around the top of the tree trunk. Begin in the crook of the tree **(Fig. 2)** and sew buttons on until the tree is full.

5. Pull the fabric tight in the hoop. Leaving about 3/4", cut off the extra fabric around the back of the hoop. Glue the fabric around the inside rim on the back of the hoop.

Fig. 1

Fig. 2

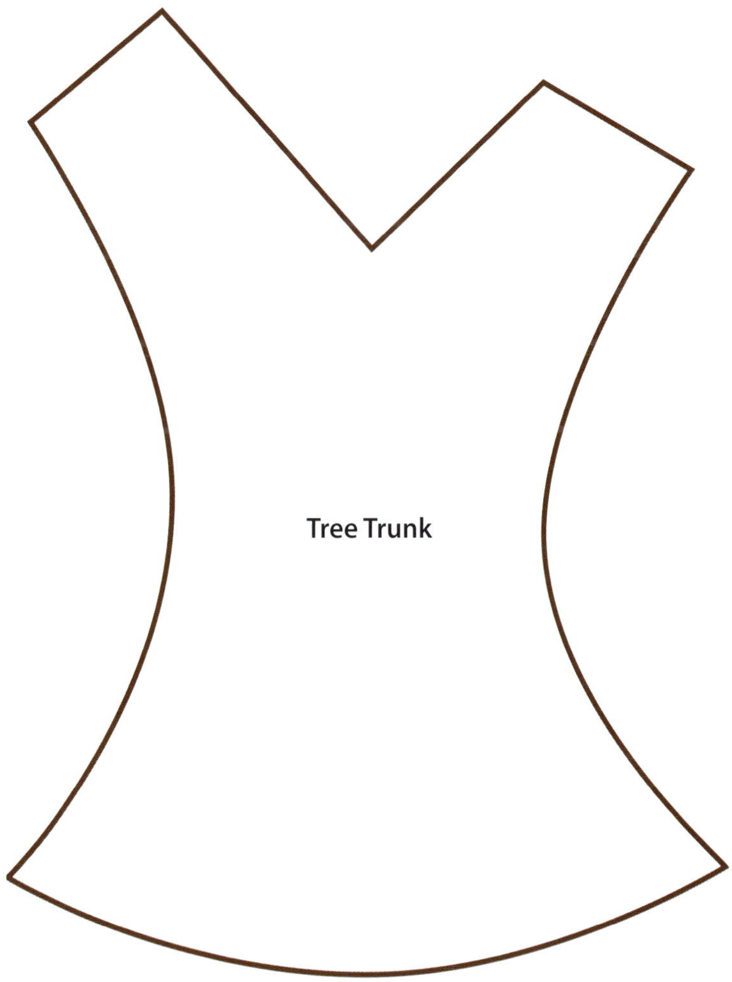

Jeans Purse

Finished Size: about 8" x 8"

SHOPPING LIST

- ❍ old pair of jeans
- ❍ paint stencil
- ❍ cardboard
- ❍ painter's tape
- ❍ acrylic paints in desired colors
- ❍ paper plate
- ❍ small foam stencil brushes
- ❍ variegated yarn
- ❍ embroidery needle with large eye
- ❍ scissors

To make the Purse

Use needle and yarn for all sewing. See ***Tip****, page 3, to knot yarn ends.*

1. Cut 8" off the bottom of 1 jeans leg. The hem of the jeans leg will be the top of the purse.

2. Place a piece of cardboard inside the leg with the seams on the sides. With the hem at the top, tape the stencil on the front of the leg (**Fig. 1**). Use the stencil brushes to paint the different areas of the stencil the way you like. Carefully remove the stencil and let the paint dry really well.

3. Remove the cardboard. Fold the leg wrong side out and lay flat.

4. Cut about 24" of yarn. To sew the bottom closed, start on 1 side of the bottom edge and bring the needle up from the bottom through both layers of the leg. Bring the needle up from the bottom through both layers again close to the first stitch. Keep stitching across the bottom of the purse with the stitches close together. This will make the purse bottom extra strong. When you reach the other side, knot the yarn; trim the extra yarn (**Fig. 2**). Turn the purse right side out.

5. To make the handle, cut twelve 36" yarn lengths. Place 1 end of each length together and tie a knot about 3" from the ends. (If you'd like longer fringe on the sides of the purse, cut the yarn longer and tie the knot farther from the ends.) Tape the knot to a table. Divide the yarn into 3 sections with 4 yarns each (**Fig. 3**). Braid the sections together. When you get near the end of the yarns, tie a knot, leaving about 3" of fringe at the ends.

6. Cut a 12" yarn length. Place 1 knot of the braided handle on 1 side of the purse below the hem. Sew the knot in place with several stitches in the same manner as Step 4. Knot the yarn; trim the extra yarn. Repeat to attach the other knot to the other side of the purse.

Fig. 1

Fig. 2

Fig. 3

Movable Head Turtle

Finished Size: about 6 1/2" x 8 1/2"

SHOPPING LIST

- ❍ craft foam - brown & green
- ❍ green yarn
- ❍ $7^1/_2$" long jumbo craft stick
- ❍ white paper
- ❍ felt-tip black permanent marker
- ❍ embroidery needle with a large eye
- ❍ googly eyes
- ❍ straight pins
- ❍ scissors
- ❍ low-temp glue gun & glue sticks
- ❍ tracing paper

To make the Turtle

*Use needle and yarn for all sewing. See **Tip**, page 3, to knot yarn ends.*

1. Trace the patterns, page 20, onto tracing paper. Use the patterns to cut 2 brown shells, 4 green feet, and 1 green head and body from craft foam.

2. Glue the head and body to the craft stick. Glue the googly eyes to the head. Use permanent marker to draw 2 nostrils on the head.

3. Glue the feet to the sides of 1 shell. Set these pieces aside.

4. Trace the hexagon pattern, page 20, onto white paper; cut out. Place the pattern in the center of the remaining shell. Using the permanent marker, draw around the shape. Leaving a small space in between, use the pattern to draw 1 hexagon on each side of the center hexagon.

5. Using the needle, poke a hole at each corner of each hexagon. Refer to **Figs. 1a-1b** and use the holes you made to sew the outlines of the hexagons on the shell. Knot the yarn on the back; trim the extra yarn.

6. Place the sewn shell on top of the remaining shell. Place the head and body in between the two shells. Use a few pins on the outside edges of the circles to hold them together.

7. Bring the needle up from the bottom of the shell on one side of the head. Sew Running Stitches **(Fig. 2)** along the outside edge of the circle until you reach the tail. Knot the yarn on the back; trim the extra yarn. Repeat for the opposite side of the shell.

8. To play with the turtle, hold the end of the tail with 1 hand and hold the shell with your other hand. Pull the turtle's tail and the head disappears into its shell. Push the turtle's tail and the head pops out of its shell **(Fig. 3)**!

Fig. 1a

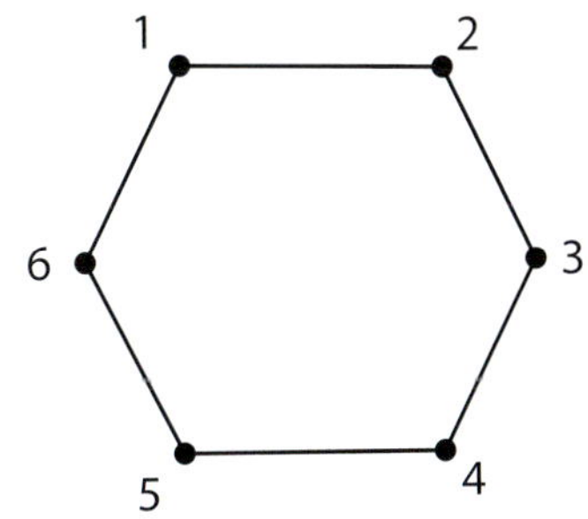

Come up at 1, down at 2, up at 3, down at 2, up at 4, down at 3, up at 5, down at 4, up at 6, down at 5, up at 1, down at 6. Move to another hexagon and come up at 1. Repeat this sequence for the remaining hexagons.

Fig. 1b

Fig. 2

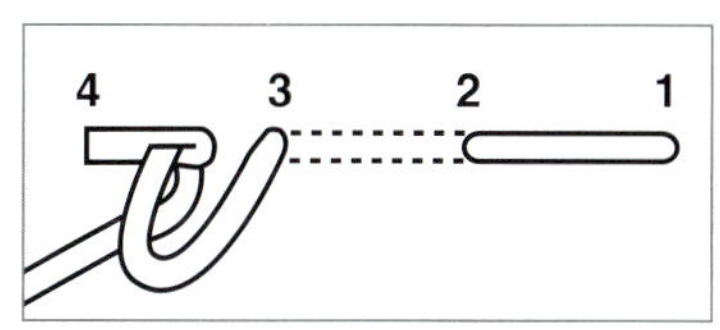

A Running Stitch consists of a series of straight stitches with the stitch length equal to the space between the stitches. Come up at 1 and go down at 2. Come up at 3 and go down at 4. Continue in this manner.

Fig. 3

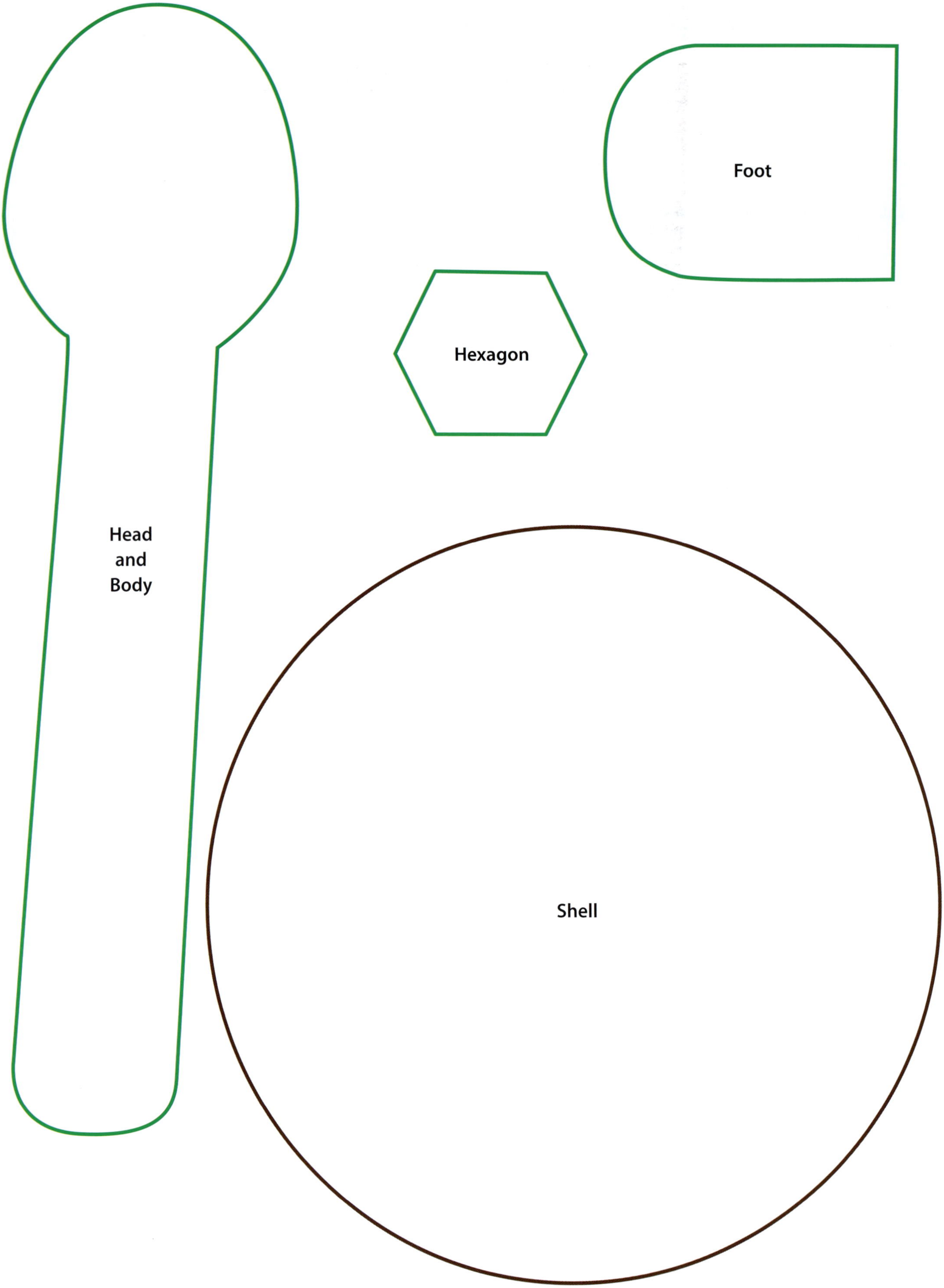
Head
and
Body
Hexagon
Foot
Shell

Jellyfish Finger Puppet

Finished Size: 1 3/4" wide x 5" long

Fig. 1

Fig. 2

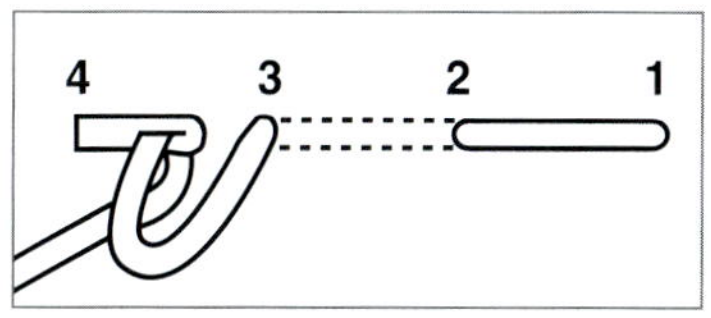

A Running Stitch consists of a series of straight stitches with the stitch length equal to the space between the stitches. Come up at 1 and go down at 2. Come up at 3 and go down at 4. Continue in this manner.

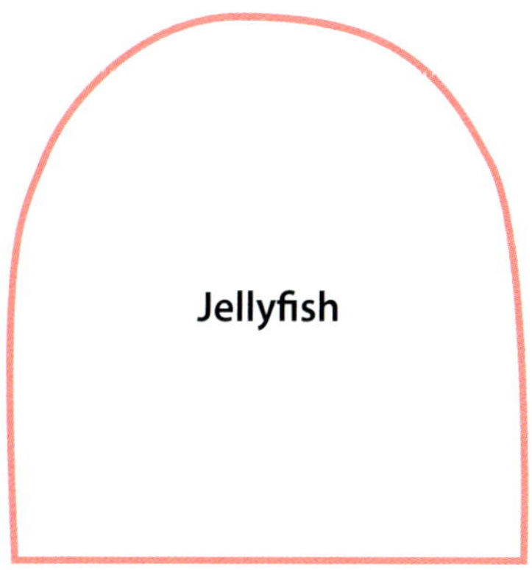

SHOPPING LIST

Note: *Supplies and instructions are for making 1 puppet.*

- ❍ desired color felt
- ❍ variegated yarn
- ❍ 2 googly eyes
- ❍ white 6-strand embroidery floss
- ❍ embroidery needle
- ❍ straight pins
- ❍ scissors
- ❍ low-temp glue gun and glue sticks
- ❍ tracing paper

To make the Puppet

Use needle and 4 strands of floss for all sewing. Knot 1 end of the floss. See ***Tip****, page 3, to knot floss ends.*

1. Trace pattern onto tracing paper. Use the pattern to cut 2 jellyfish from felt.
2. Cut 24 3" lengths of yarn. Lay the jellyfish pieces down. Glue 12 pieces to the bottom of each piece **(Fig. 1)**.
3. Pin the jellyfish pieces together with the yarn ends inside. Starting at the bottom of the jellyfish, use Running Stitches **(Fig. 2)** to sew around the jellyfish. Knot the floss on the back; trim the extra floss.
4. Glue the googly eyes to the jellyfish.
5. To play with your jellyfish, open the bottom of the body and place it on your finger with the yarn tentacles surrounding your finger. Now watch the jellyfish glide as you move your finger.

Photo Frame

Finished Size: about 8" x 8"

SHOPPING LIST

Note: *Supplies and instructions are for making 1 photo frame.*

- ❍ 4 jumbo craft sticks
- ❍ variegated yarn in desired color
- ❍ mini clothespin
- ❍ 10" of jute
- ❍ low-temp glue gun and glue sticks

To make the Photo Frame

1. Overlapping the ends, glue the craft sticks together in a square.
2. Cut a long strand of yarn. Glue 1 end of the yarn on the back in 1 corner of 1 of the craft sticks (**Fig. 1**).
3. Wrap the yarn tightly around the craft stick, continuing until you reach the opposite corner. Glue the yarn onto the back of the stick; cut off any extra.
4. Repeat Step 3, wrapping yarn around all 4 craft sticks.
5. Glue the ends of the jute on the back of the top two corners of the frame.
6. Glue the clothespin on the center front at the top of the frame.
7. Hang the frame on the wall with the jute. Hang your photo from the clothespin. A 4" x 4" photo works best.

Fig. 1

Owl Purse

Finished Size: about 6 1/2" wide x 20" long

SHOPPING LIST

***Note:** Supplies and instructions are for making 1 purse.*

- felt - white, black, orange, and 2 other colors of your choice
- 30" of 1" wide lace
- 6-strand embroidery floss - white and colors of your choice
- embroidery needle
- straight pins
- air-soluble fabric marker
- scissors
- tracing paper

To make the Purse

*Use needle and 6 strands of floss for all sewing. Knot 1 end of the floss. See **Tip**, page 3, to knot floss ends.*

1. Trace patterns, page 24, onto tracing paper. Use the patterns to cut 2 desired color bodies, 2 desired color wings, 2 white large eyes, 2 black pupils, and 1 orange beak from felt.

2. Use the marker to draw 3 rows of zigzag lines on each wing. Use desired color floss and refer to **Fig. 1** to sew over the drawn lines. Knot the floss on the back; trim the extra floss.

3. Pin the eyes, pupils, beak, and wings to 1 body. Using white floss and Running Stitches **(Fig. 2)**, sew the pieces to the body. Knot the floss on the back; trim the extra floss.

4. Place the stitched body on top of the remaining body; pin. Pin 2" of the ribbon ends between the layers on each side at the top of the purse **(Fig. 3, page 24)**.

5. Thread the needle with white floss; knot the other end. Using white floss and Running Stitches, sew the body pieces together, catching the ribbon in the stitching at the top. Knot the floss on the inside; trim the extra floss.

Fig. 1

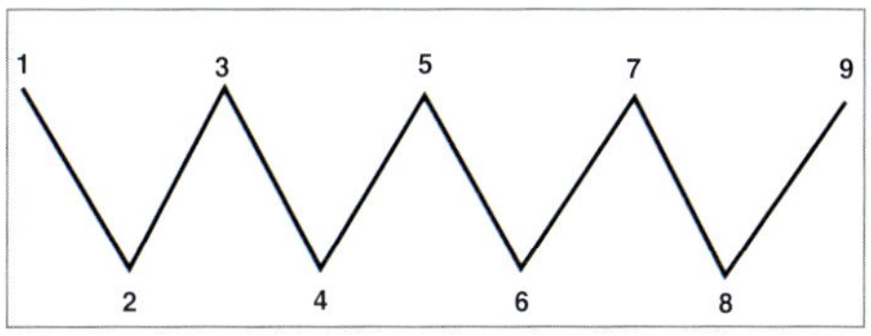

Come up at 1; go down at 2. Come up at 3; go down at 2. Come up at 4; go down at 3. Come up at 5; go down at 4. Continue in this manner.

Fig. 2

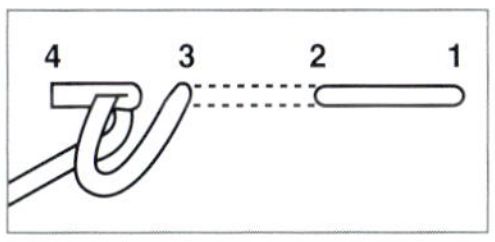

A Running Stitch consists of a series of straight stitches with the stitch length equal to the space between the stitches. Come up at 1 and go down at 2. Come up at 3 and go down at 4. Continue in this manner.

Fig. 3

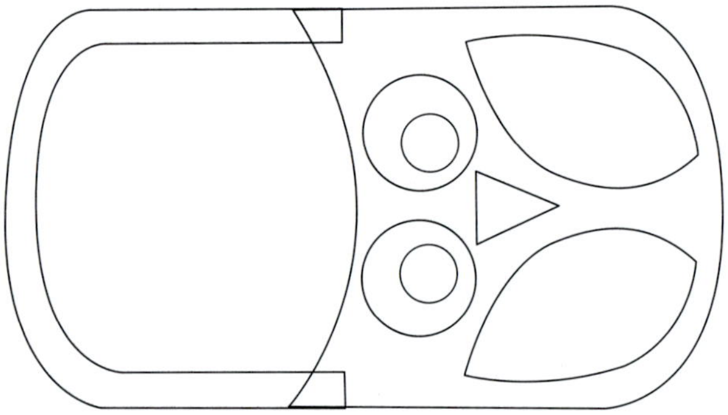

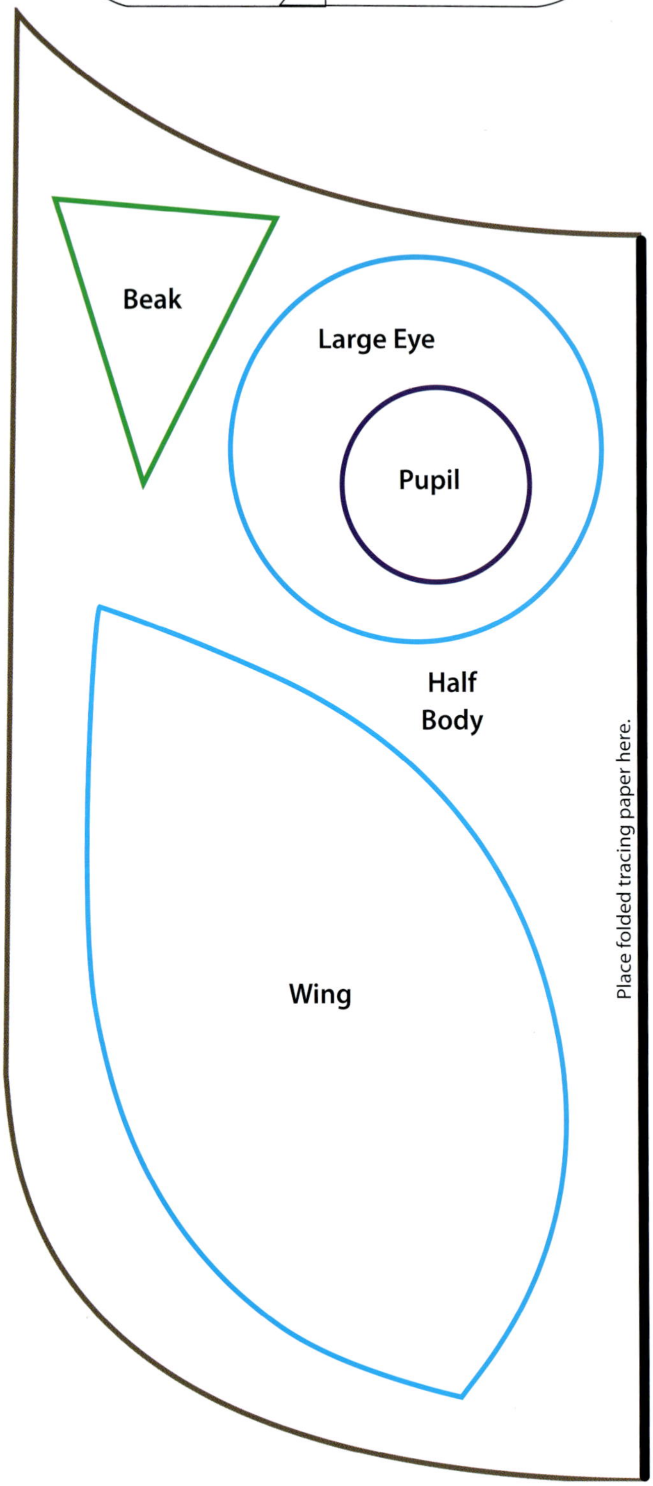

Meet Rachel Nipper

Fond memories of childhood creativity are the driving force behind Rachel Nipper's love of arts and crafts.

A mother of two sons and a daughter, Rachel enjoys passing along playful and colorful ideas to her children and to other parents and educators.

"My children are my main drive and inspiration. I love to create projects that align with their interests and hobbies or that go along with activities we do together as a family."

Rachel says all of the designs in this book have a useful component to them, as you can either play with them after creating them, display them as décor, or use them on a day-to-day basis.

For more about Rachel, visit her website, www.iheartcraftythings.com, to find fun and simple activities for children, educational activities, printables, and creative family fun ideas.

Production Team: Technical Writer – Lisa Lancaster; Technical Associate – Mary Sullivan Hutcheson; Editorial Writer – Susan Frantz Wiles; Senior Graphic Artist – Lora Puls; Graphic Artist – Kellie McAnulty; Photostylist – Lori Wenger; Photographer – Jason Masters.